THE ANT, THE PLANT, AND THE CATERPILLAR

A story about the lifecycle of the
Eltham Copper Butterfly and a very special friendship.

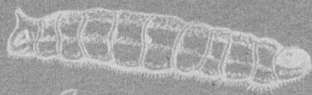

Caterpillar

Bursaria flower

Sweet Bursaria flower

Notoncus ant

Bursaria Leaf

Sweet Bursaria leaves

seed pods

Notoncus ant

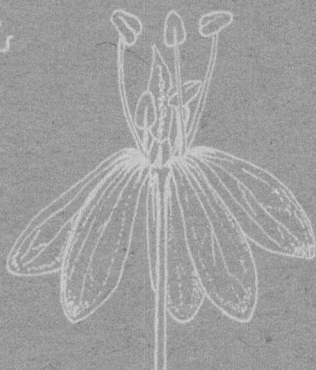

Bursaria Leaf

Bursaria flower

Notoncus ant

Caterpillar

seed pods

Caterpillar

Bursaria Leaf

Bursaria flower

ant

THIS BOOK BELONGS TO:

....

....

Sweet Bursaria
leaves

Sweet Bursaria
flower

seed pods

Bursaria Leaf

FOR ALL THE LITTLE CONSERVATIONISTS IN THE WORLD

The author acknowledges the support of the Banyule City Council, Victoria
through the Enviornmental Grant scheme.

Hardccover edition May 2023
Nature House Press
ISBN 978-0-6457404-0-0

Book written and illustrated by Karen Carter
www.karencarter.au

Editor Robin Griffith

in conjunction with the Efflorescence Project

Efflorescence Project.com
Botanical Design for Environmental Communications

THE ANT, THE PLANT, AND THE CATERPILLAR

Written and illustrated by
Karen Carter

Dedicated to Emsie,
my friend, colleague, and supervisor whose constant support I could not
repay. Without our frank banter this book may not have launched.
Forever grateful for you.

It was a hot, dry summer afternoon in the woodlands of Greenhills. The sun was starting to drop behind the towering Yellow Box gum trees. In the distance, Kookaburras laughed while green Swift parrots darted through the treetops.

Elouera, the Eltham Copper Butterfly, was flitting between bushes, looking for a familiar plant upon which to lay her eggs.

Finally, Elouera found the native Sweet Bursaria bush she was looking for. This was her family plant. It was where she had been born, and her mother before her, and her mother before her.

Elouera knew her eggs would be safe, for beneath the plant, deep under the ground, there lived the Notoncus ants. The Notoncus ants had long been friends – and fierce protectors of – the Eltham Copper Butterfly.

Notoncus capitatus ant

Elouera laid her eggs on a leaf at the bottom of their family plant. The Notoncus ants scurried to the surface to watch the event, and so did Mr Inky Prickles, the local Echidna who lived nearby.

Elouera looked at her beloved babies for the last time and told them she loved them. Then, she flew away into the evening sky. Her job was done. Now, they were in the care of the Notoncus ants.

*Eltham Copper Butterfly eggs laid on
a Sweet Bursaria spinosa leaf.*

FUN FACT: Without the Sweet Bursaria plant and the Notoncus ants, the Eltham Copper Butterfly could not survive. They need the plant for food and the ants to house and protect them.

Did you know? Mr Inky Prickles doesn't eat this family of ants, he is their friend.

One young ant named Nathan was very excited as this was his first time raising a caterpillar. He waited and waited for the eggs to hatch until one morning, a munching sound woke him. Nathan scurried up the plant. He blinked his eyes. Could it be? Yes, it was! A baby caterpillar was chewing its way out of its shell.

"Good morning," the baby caterpillar said, blinking at Nathan, "My name is Lucida."

"My name is Nathan, and I am your personal guard," said Nathan as he puffed out his chest proudly. "I am sure we will be great friends and I have so much to tell you, come along, let's go to my nest underground, it's safe and warm." They made their way down the Sweet Bursaria bush into the ant nest.

Caterpillar emerging from the egg
on a Sweet Bursaria spinosa leaf.

In the nest, Nathan and Lucida talked and talked. He told her things his father had taught him and that when she was ready, they would go up to the surface so she could eat as many Sweet Bursaria leaves as she liked to make her big and strong.

He told her that after she eats the leaves, she makes a delicious sweet juice from her back. Ants love it. Nathan asked Lucida if she would share some delicious juice with him. Lucida happily agreed. She would give it to Nathan as a reward for protecting her.

"However, we still have to be very careful, as there are many predators that may want to eat you Lucida," said Nathan. Lucida became a little frightened. "Do not worry," Nathan reassured her. "I will be with you all the time; I won't let anything happen to you."

Predators

Huntsman Spider
Sparassidae

European Wasp
Vespula germanica

Lucida was very excited when it came time to feed on the Sweet Bursaria bush. As night fell, Nathan and the female ants rode on Lucida's back, guiding her up the branches. She munched on the leaves. "How delicious!" she declared.

While Lucida was feeding, Nathan saw the 'Huntsman' spider hiding in the branches one evening. He was waiting for Lucida to come closer so he could gobble her up. Nathan jumped into action. "Hurry Lucida!" He pushed the growing caterpillar down the plant. "We must get you into the nest," shouted Nathan. "It's not safe, there are too many predators tonight."

They quickly made their way down into the nest. Lucida sighed, "Oh thank you Nathan, you are the greatest friend a caterpillar could have."

All through Winter and early Spring, Lucida ate all she could eat. Now, it was time she rested and went into her cocoon. It was time to pupate.

"Goodnight, Nathan," Lucida yawned as she spun her cocoon around her. "Good night, Lucida," said Nathan. "I will be here watching over you and waiting until you wake up."
Before long, she was all wrapped up and sound asleep.

As Summer approached and the air outside became warmer and drier, the flowers began to bloom on the Sweet Bursaria bushes. Nathan knew their time together would end, and he would have to say goodbye to his special friend.

Sweet Bursaria spinosa flowering

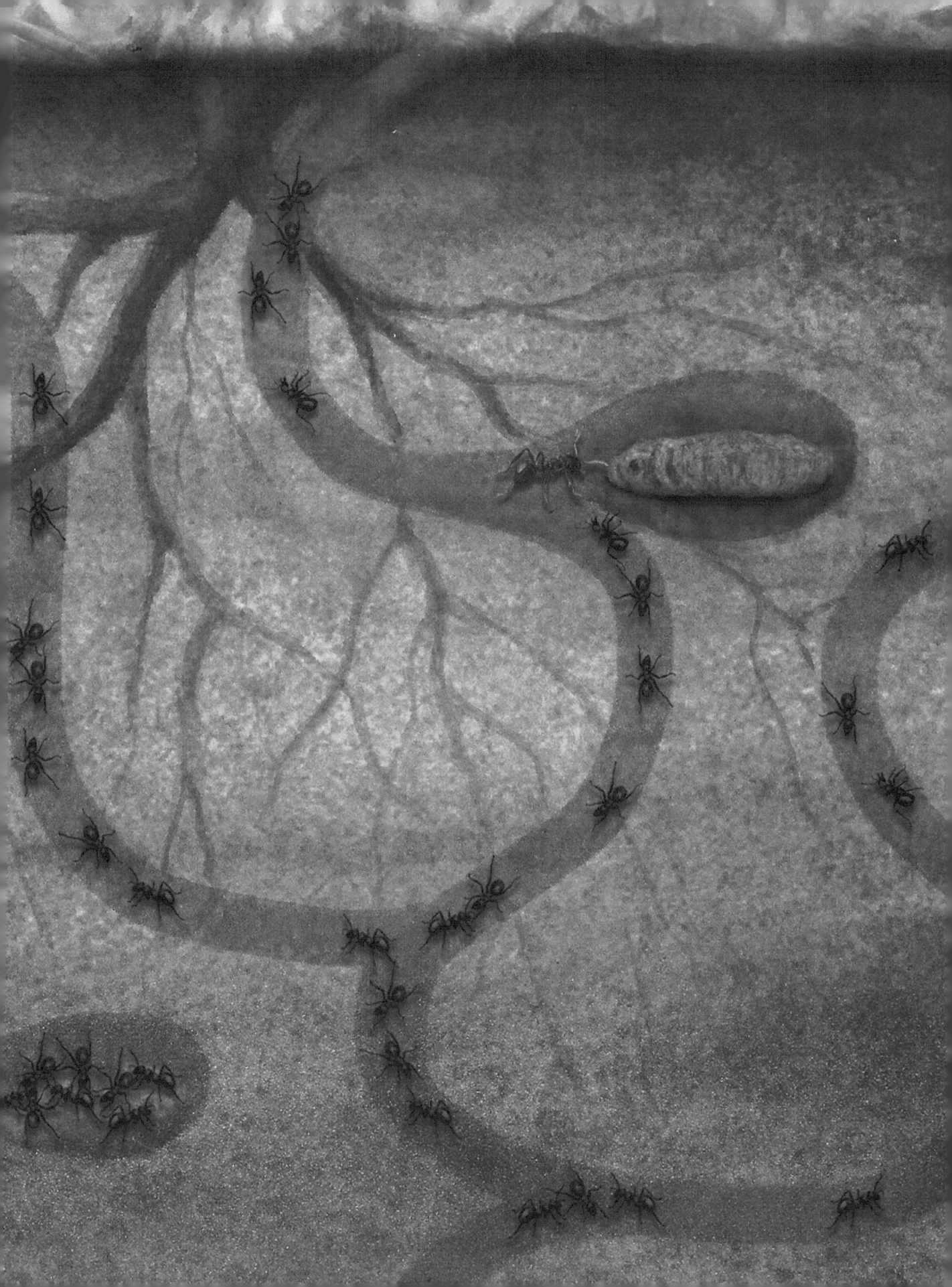

One hot summer morning, Nathan woke to find Lucida had gone.
He looked everywhere, but he could not find her. His heart was racing.
"Lucida!" he called.
"Up here Nathan," Lucida excitedly replied, "look at me!"
Nathan looked up. Flitting in circles, a beautiful copper-coloured
butterfly was up in the sky. "Lucida," he exclaimed, "is that you?"
"Yes, it's me," Lucida laughed. Then she flew down to Nathan and
landed on the plant.

He looked down sadly and softly said, "It is time for you to leave, isn't it?" "Yes," replied Lucida.

She flew up into the sky and hovered over the little ant. "Goodbye Nathan, I will never forget you, you are my best friend," she said. Nathan shouted, "I will never forget you either, Lucida." And away Lucida flew. "Goodbye, Nathan ant ... goodbye," Her voice started fading.

Nathan smiled as Lucida, the Eltham Copper Butterfly, flew off into the sky. He knew he would never see her again, but he would be there to raise her babies when the time came. And the cycle would begin again.

Eltham Copper Butterfly
Paralucia pyrodiscus lucida

LEARN MORE.........

The Eltham Copper Butterfly is an insect species at risk of becoming extinct and disappearing forever. The species is classified as an Endangered Invertebrate in Victoria because of the loss of its bush habitat, the land where the butterfly lives.

This is due to urbanisation, which means building houses, shops, and roads. Other reasons are weed invasion, people dumping rubbish and walking on the plants, cutting down the plants, and bushfires. Agriculture (which is farming) has also caused the loss of the butterfly habitat. If the Eltham Copper Butterfly becomes extinct, it could affect biodiversity by upsetting the delicate balance in nature.

How big is the Eltham Copper Butterfly?

The butterfly is tiny, the size of a coin, just over one centimetre. It is not easy to see the butterfly flitting amongst the Sweet Bursaria plants because it is pretty fast. Its grey wings on the underside make it hard to see, as it blends with the plants.

1.94CM

Where is the butterfly found?

The Eltham Copper Butterfly is found only in small pockets in Victoria.

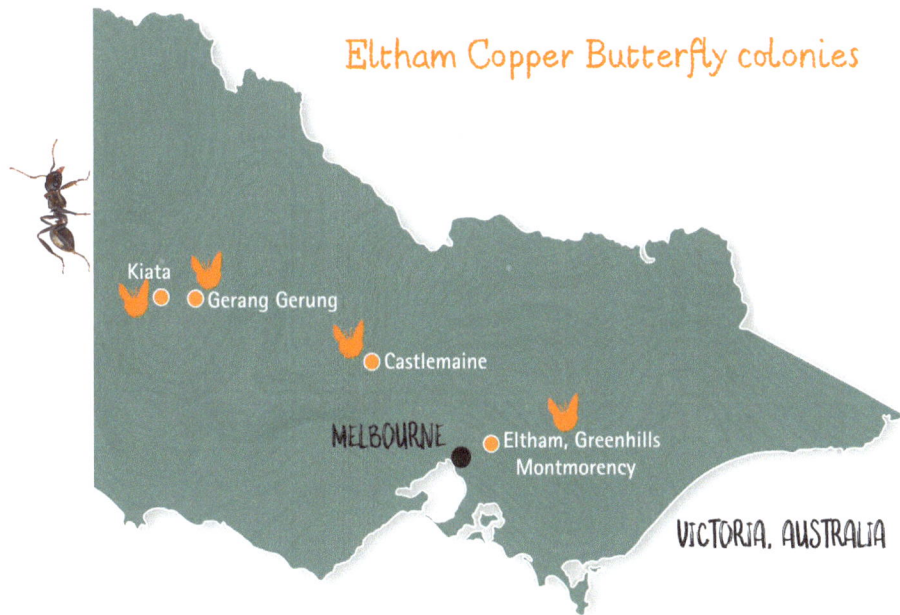

Eltham Copper Butterfly colonies

Kiata
Gerang Gerung
Castlemaine
MELBOURNE
Eltham, Greenhills
Montmorency
VICTORIA, AUSTRALIA

HOW CAN WE HELP THE ELTHAM COPPER BUTTERFLY?

In these areas where the Eltham Copper Butterfly still lives, we can help protect the habitats by looking after the Sweet Bursaria plant and ensuring we keep the bush reserves clear of rubbish and weeds. We need to walk on the paths, not on or through the plants. We can participate by counting caterpillars at night in Spring when they come out of the ant nests to feed on the Sweet Bursaria plant. Counting caterpillars helps organisations to know if the butterfly is surviving well.

Most of all, we can tell our friends and family how important it is to save precious species like the Eltham Copper Butterfly for our planet.

Sweet Bursaria flower

Bursaria flower

Bursaria Leaf

Sweet Bursaria leaves

Bursaria Leaf

ECB

Copper Butterfly

Bursaria flower

Bu

ECB

Bursaria Leaf

Bursaria flower

Copper Butterfly

Sweet Bursaria
leaves

Sweet Bursaria
flower

Sweet Bursaria
leaves

ECB

af

Bursaria Leaf

ELTHAM COPPER BUTTERFLY QUIZ

1. What season do the Eltham Copper Butterflies lay their eggs?

2. Where is the Eltham Copper Butterfly found?

3. What plant do the caterpillars eat?

4. Where do the caterpillars live during winter?

5. Who guards the caterpillars?

6. Who are the preditors of the caterpillars?

7. What reward do the Notoncus ants receive?

8. What season do the caterpillars turn into Butterflies?

9. How big is the Eltham Copper Butterfly?

10. What colour are the wings of the Eltham Copper Butterfly?

EXTRA: How can people help the Eltham Copper Butterflies survive?

To learn more about the Eltham Copper Butterfly and to access teaching notes and activities, please visit my website: karencarter.au

www.ingramcontent.com/pod-product-compliance
Lightning Source LLC
Chambersburg PA
CBHW041548260326
41914CB00016B/1583